The Lost Gospel: A Text, Translation and Commentary

By

Howard Leigh

MMXX

New Platonist Collective
Publishing

ISBN: 978-1-8381496-4-2
A CIP catalogue record for this book is available from the British Library

Introduction

Forasmuch as this gospel has been lost for millenia, it is my pleasure to present it to the world.

Suppressed by ecclesial authorities, now pieced together from original sources through painstaking research - my painstaking research - the Lost Gospel exposes the reality of Jesus of Nazareth for the first time. Here you will find the original story in all of its juiciness and flavour. It is a groundbreaking breakthrough in knowledge, and if it doesn't win me the Scott-Stott Medallion, I don't know what will. So read, and enjoy. This will change your life.

I present a threefold work: the original text, my translation and a commentary. This publication is not uncontroversial. Is my theology is a little idiosyncratic? Is my translation is at times questionable? Am I occasionally foul-mouthed and obscene? Does my imagination and illustrative capacity carry me far from the matters at hand? Yes yes yes yes. But it is this very colour that makes this book - despite its scholarship - accessible for a general readership.

May you gain from this groundbreaking research and join my campaign to have this lost gospel recognised within the canon of scripture.

Howard Leigh
University of Dunwich
All Hallow's Eve MMXX

1 - PROLOGUE - THE HEAVENLY BANQUET

Ἐν το τελος παντων· περισσευμα ἀπο ἀνατολων και δυσμων ἥχουσιν και ἀνακλιθησονται μετα Ἀβααμ και Ἰσαακ και Ἰακοβ ἐν τη βασιλεια των οὐπανων.

το τουτο δειπνον του γαμου του ἀρνιου ἐχο περοσσος ἀριου οἰνου· γαρ Χπιστος ἐστιν ὁ ἀρτος της ζωης· ὁ ἐρχομενος προς αὐτον οὐ μη διψνσει πωποτε. ἐαν τις φαγη ἐκ τουτου του ἀρτου ζησει εἰς τον αἰωνα ὁ τρωγων αὐτου της σαρκα και πινων αὐτου το αἰμα ἐχει ζωην αἰωνιον.

θεος ἐν Χριστος ἐπερισσευσεν το πλουτος της χαριτος αὐτου. γαρ ἐκ του πληρωματος αὐτος ἡμεις παντες ἐλαβομεν και χαριτος ἀντι χαριτος. Γευσασθε και ἰδετε ὁτι χρηστος ὁ κυριος.

το δειπνον περισσον ἡτοιμαχθην· δευρο συγκαθιζε τοχαριτος πατρος και τον υἱον τον ἁγιον πνευματος. φαγε.

Translation
At the end of all things there will be a great feast of abundance and people will come from east and west to sit down with Abraham, Isaac and Jacob. This wedding feast of the Lamb has lots of bread and wine, for Christ is the bread of life. Anyone who comes to him will never want. Whoever eats the bread and drinks the wine will have eternal life: those eating the flesh and drinking the blood will have eternal life. God in Christ has caused to abound the riches of his grace. For from his fullness we all have received grace upon grace. Taste and see that the Lord is good. The abundant banquet has been prepared, come sit down with the Father, the Son and the Holy Spirit. Eat up!

Commentary
On initial reading the poor condition of the manuscript is immediately evident. The passage of time has not been kind to these ancient fragments, with accentation and subscripts lost, and a number of scribal errors. However I ask you to look beyond this, to the meaning of the text. What we see here is extraordinary. In this prologue introductory passage the striking sense is one of overflowing abundance. Words related to the Greek Periss- come 8 times. Here is the grace of God displayed.

The picture of eating will doubtless cause many to make associations with the Catholic sacramental system of salvation. In traditional Roman Catholic theology the great heavenly banquet is the Mass. However interpreting this prologue in this way misses the point slightly. More than anything else what is particularly evident is the sheer excess and generosity of this feast, and the fact that is crosses every distinctive line of identity, including ecclesial identity. What the writer seems to be saying is this: do you want to know what it means to have union with Christ? Then taste and see the surpassing sweetness of Christ's goodness.

To illustrate the point let me describe to you my research group at Cromwell College, all specialists in early-Christian writings: Devins, Crichton, Rice. It was the Christmas meal out at the local Turkish restaurant and at the end came the vexed question: how shall we divide up the bill?

Now Rice is notoriously tight-arsed when it comes to paying up. She never wants to split the bill equally, only to pay for her own individualistic consumption. As you can imagine I am an advocate of justice and equality and splitting the bill. It was their own fault that they sat there ravenous watching me masticate my starter. Devins is something of a peacemaker in these situations but recently Crichton has taken to siding with Rice in every disagreement. It was no different today. In any case, our meal highlights an enormous contrast with the heavenly banquet: God's endless generosity and abundance and grace.

2 - THE CONCEPTION OF JESUS

Μαριας μνηστευθεισης τω Ιωσηφ ἠγαπησεν Ρωμαῖος κεντυριων. και Μαριας ἐμοιχεσεν τω αυτον.

ουν εγενετο ἁπαξ ὁτε ἐμοιχεσεν αυτος λεγει φυκ ἡ θηκη ἐσεσχιζκεν. και Μαριας λεγει φυκ και ἐμβριμησατο τω πνευματι. και αυτη εγενετο ἐγκυον.

νυν ἐν τω μηνι τω ἑκτω ὁ ἀνγελος Γαβριηλ εἰσελθων προς αὐτην εἰπεν Μη φοβου Μαριαμ, εὑρες γαρ χαριν παρα τω θεω. και ιδου συλλημψη ἐν γαστρι και τεξη υἱον και καλεσεις το ὀνομα αὐτου Ἰησουν. οὑτος ἐσται μεγας και υἱος ὑψιστου κληθησεται και δωσει αὐτω κυριος ὁ θεος τον θρονον Δαυιδ του πατρος αυτου.

Ιωσηφ δε ὁ ἀνερ αὐτης, δικαιος ὠν και μη θελων αὐτεν δειγματισαι, ἐβουληθη λαθπα ἀπολυσαι. ταυτα δε αὐτου ἐνθυμηθεντος ἰδου ἀγγελος κυριου κατ' ὀναρ ἐφανη αὐτω λεγων, μη φοβηθης παραλαβειν Μαριαν της γυναικα σου· το γαρ ἐν αὐτη γεννεθεν ἐκ θελω θεου.

Translation

It came to be that Mary, having been engaged to Joseph, loved a Roman Centurion. And they committed adultery. Now, one night whilst they were committing adultery, he said:
'Lo! The sheath has split open,' And Mary said 'Lo!' and was greatly troubled in spirit. And she became pregnant. Now in the third month the angel Gabriel came to Mary and said: 'Don't be afraid Mary, you have found grace from God. And behold, the baby in your tummy will be called Jesus. This baby will be great and will be called son of the Highest and the Lord God will give him the throne of David his father.' Joseph, her husband, being a just man and unwilling to humiliate her, wanted to release her discreetly. But as he ruminated on this, behold an angel of the

Lord appeared in a dream, saying: 'do not be afraid to take up Mary as your wife. For the foetus in her is of God's will.'

Commentary

Here we see that Jesus was not born of a virgin, but illegitimately in a carnal manner.

committing adultery - Devins, of course, refuses to admit the authenticity of this fragment, the puritanical turd. It is easy to see why it has been repressed by church authorities ever since it was written. However that Jesus was born from a vaginal conception should not be considered a barrier to his meaning and significance, but rather a deepening of it. Here, what pathos, that the Christ was the illegitimate son of a bit of rumpy-pumpy. What hope it gives to all outcasts and sex-freaks.

Son of the Most High - Now is probably a good moment to mention the Trinity. One can easily imagine the embarrassment for the Jewish follower of Jesus as a strict monotheist in the first century. In the earliest proclamation Jesus is described as taking on roles which only God is meant to have: forgiving, bringing salvation, operating with God's own authority. He is presented as God's own Son. Worship of Jesus naturally bubbles up within the proto-Christians. Before they have thought it through, they are treating Jesus as divine. And it doesn't stop there. For although God and Jesus were not physically present with them, they felt as if they were. Moreover, things kept on happening that convinced them that God was active among them and within them: that he had put his own Spirit in their hearts, another element of the divine. It is awkward to the monotheist for divinity to multiply like this. We can easily see what a mess they got themselves into, a mess which later theologians such as Arius attempted to extricate the church from, unsuccessfully. How much easier to say at the outset that Jesus was not divine in any literal sense. Surely the virgin birth was simply invented after the event, as proved by this passage. As for Devins who claims that if Jesus was not divine then the whole edifice of salvation falls, I say, let it fall.

divorce her quietly - when my wife divorced me it certainly was not quietly, but then she was not a quiet woman.

3 - THE BIRTH OF JESUS

Μαριαμ και Ἰωσηφ ανεβη εκ πολεως Ναζαρεθ εις πολιν Βηθλεεμ ἀντι Καισαρου Αυγουστου ἐχῆλθεν δογμα ἀπογραφεσθαι πᾶσαν την οἰκουμενην.

ἐν δυσβαστακτος μεσος χειμων· ψῦχος ἀνεμος ἀνακραζω. ἡ γῆ ὡς σιδηρος και ὑδωρ ὡς λιθος. χιων ἐπεσεν· χιων ἀντι χιων. ἐν δυσβαστακτος μεσος χειμων παλαι.

ὀλιγον ὀναριον επι χοῦς ὁδος δεῖ προσκαρτερειν συν σος πολυτιμος βαρος δει βασταζειν Μαριαμ ἐκσωζειν εις Βηθλεεμ.

ὀλιγος πολις Βηθλεεμ ἐζήτησαν καταλυμα. πρωτος καταλυματι οὐκ ἦν αὐτοις τοπος· δευτεροπρωτος καταλυματι οὐκ ἦν αὐτοις τοπος· τριτος καταλυματι ἐαει αυτοις ἐπιμενειν ἐν αυτου νομὰς . ἐκει ἐτεκεν τω βπεφω και ανεκλινεν αυτον ἐν φατνη.

ὁτε ποιμενες ἐπλυνον αυτων πους ἐσθνς της νυκτος, παντες ἐκάθισουσιν παρα νιπηρι, και ἀγγελος κυριου πεπιελαμψεν, και ἐκαθισαν αυτων πουσἐσθνς.

ἡμεις τρεις βασιλεις ἀνατολου ἐσμεν βασταζομεν δωροι και ὁδευομεν μακραν.

Translation

Mary and Joseph went up from the town of Nazareth to the city of Bethlehem since Caesar Augustus has issued a decree that all the world be registered. In the difficult wintery months the cold winds blew and the ground was hard with frost and the water was frozen solid. Lots of snow fell. A little donkey carried Mary and her precious baby along the poorly maintained roads until they reached Bethlehem. In David's city they looked for a place to stay. The first inn was full, as was the second. The third innkeeper let them stay in his stable. There she gave birth to the baby and laid him in a manger. Now while shepherds watched their flocks by night all seated on the ground, the angel of the Lord came down, and glory shone around. Similarly there were three kings who travelled from the orient, bearing gifts.

Donkey...snow...innkeepers...stable...three kings...
Here is dramatic proof that the parochial English traditions of Christmas are based on a venerable tradition.

A lot of work has been done recently in showing the resilience of verbal tradition operating alongside written records. In regard to the Christmas story we see here an independent verbal tradition, rooted in my text, that surfaces through the centuries at various points. This hidden tradition has been kept alive in stories passed down from parent to child, but now are given scholarly backing for the first time. It will be a great encouragement to all who enjoy Christmas, that these traditions that we enjoy are originally based upon a document from earliest times. I remember the Nativity plays of my own children. There they are with their milky reek and disarming curls in the green pastel painted school hall, with creaky scenery and creakier singing; their costumes, one year a floppy sheep's ear, another a tree, the next a wailing angel who has broken her halo; the forgotten lines and long pauses and burning pride; the fittingness of having children exegete a baby saviour; tasting again the immediacy of childhood through the confusion and wonder of my own children; and all suffused by that undefinable glow: whether from the giftbright expectation of shining eyes and rosy cheeks, or some primal ache of collective warmth in the darkness of midwinter, or bitter-sweetness of nostalgia - happiness reconstructed and lost.

It has been years since I saw those children.

Straining the memory further, one recalls the Christmas plays of my own youth. In the dim lit church, my progression through the roles until one year I took the part of Joseph. I had to kiss Mary.

Nativity Plays are not commonly composed by major theologians. They should be mandatory, and would cut through some major arse-waff in the academic conveyer-belt. The closest publication available is the dialogue produced by Schleiermacher *On Christmas Eve.* As a Nativity Play it is fairly crap but we will forgive him that is it is intended more as a Socratic dialogue. Still, it is a fictional performance set at Christmas time about the incarnation, and so we will call it a Nativity Play. In it Schleiermacher describes the Christmas Eve festivities of a family and their friends, with the children, women and men offering varying perspectives on Christmas. What emerges is that for Schleiermacher the emphasis in Christmas is upon the subjective feeling that it produces: the joy and love of the event. There is an Enlightenment turning to the subject here, but rather than this producing a rationalistic dissection of doctrine there is a celebration of the experience in the believer. And so Schleiermacher can remain elusive over whether he regards the incarnation allegorically or literally.

Schleiermacher definitely wants to keep the underlying theological meaning of the incarnation, but he doesn't have the balls to wade into the debate over whether it actually happened. He very much wants to leave behind any historical claims and put the focus on the present: the manger as myth. The result is, unfortunately, some useless waffle that convinces no-one except effeminate Anglican clergy. Far better to be clear and honest. Take Athanasius for example, he knows what he is talking about: "God became man in order that man might become divine." For Athanasius, God really did take on human nature in its fullness in Christ, so that humans might therefore be united to the divine essence. Previously God was distant and unknown, now he is close. God himself came to enter our reality and carry us back with him into glory. Athanasius is not hedging his bets. Of course he is entirely mistaken, but at least we know what he is saying. The incarnation is a ridiculous idea. Even if I sometimes cry during Carol Services.

4 - BAPTISM

και ἐγενετο ἐν ἐκειναις ταις ἡμεραις ἐλθεν Ἰησους ἀπο Ναζαρετ της Γαλιλαιας και ἐβαπτισθη ἐις τον Ἰορδανην ὑπο Ιωαννου. και τους οὐρανους σχιζμενους και το πνουμα ὡς περιστεραν καταβαινον εἰς αὐτον. και ἡ περιστερα ποιει κοπρον επι αυτον.

Translation
And it came to be that Jesus came out from Nazareth in Galillee and was baptised by John in the river Jordan. And the heavens split open and the Spirit of God descended on him like a pigeon. And the Spirit blessed him.

Commentary
It is always a crucial period, the entry into a public role. Questions of legitimacy and authority hover in the background. Jesus' own baptism in all accounts functions to seal his status as God's Son.

Not all public ministry begins so auspiciously. For instance, John Wesley's public ministry began in mental torture. As can be seen from his journals, he vacillated between confidence and despair in his standing before God, even after his supposed conversion at Aldersgate; after this event he still was cast into agonies concerning whether he was good enough. The breakthrough moment came when his ministry became successful. When he saw the crowd and the appreciative way they responded to him, his faith was validated. He was finally happy and at peace.

The psychologist Ian Lovecock tells us that we only believe that we are worthwhile when others see us as such and reflect this back to us. We need success and outside affirmation to feel good about ourselves. Otherwise we live in fear of everyone, because any single person can rip us to shreds with a devastating put down.

One element of baptism is that it functions as a badge of communion with God. It is that external means which can show an inward reality, and even through its subjective effect actually brings about that reality. To illustrate from my own life, in 5F in Junior School I was appointed by Mrs Farrow as Board Monitor. But my newfound status and lordship were resented by the remainder of the class. One playtime they surrounded me and shouted insults at me: board-bastard, suck-up, misery-monitor. I came to Mrs Farrow and explained why I had to resign the position. Yes it was an important role but I could not take the pressure. I abjured her to appoint officious Arnold in my place: he would perform almost adequately. I remember her words in reply very clearly:

"I am glad that you came to talk to me about this. Just today I have received a Badge of Honour in the post from Princess Anne."

"Badge of Honour?"

"As board monitor you are indirectly an officer of the crown. This is a mark of your membership of an elite. Howard, this is the sign to everyone that you are a person of distinction and that you are good enough."

The badge lay there in her palm, blue with silver lettering. I decided to rescind my resignation and have worn the Badge of Honour every day since.

5 - TEMPTATION

> καν'τ βη αρσεδ το ωριτε ανυ μορε Γρεεκ ριγτ νοω. καν'τ βη αρσεδ το ωριτε ανυ μορε Γρεεκ ριγτ νοω. καν'τ βη αρσεδ το ωριτε ανυ μορε Γρεεκ ριγτ νοω. καν'τ βη αρσεδ το ωριτε ανυ μορε Γρεεκ ριγτ νοω. καν'τ βη αρσεδ το ωριτε ανυ μορε Γρεεκ ριγτ νοω. καν'τ βη αρσεδ το ωριτε ανυ μορε Γρεεκ ριγτ νοω.

Translation
And the Spirit drove Jesus into the wilderness and there the Devil tempted him.

Commentary
Rice runs to work every day and is an aficionado of lycra. She takes it all rather seriously. Training for something or other. All a bit sweaty and hot if you ask me.

As she was stretching down one day Crichton and I were waiting in line outside the office for our caffeine hit from the booth there.
'Will you be going for the doughnut again today?' I asked.
'I wasn't going to, but seeing it there I think I will,' he said.
'Here, hold this,' he said handing me the doughnut whilst he paid.
'Tempting to take a bite,' I said.
'Yes,' he said, 'it raises some philosophical questions over the psychology of temptation doesn't it?'
'It's just a doughnut.' Meanwhile Rice's tight arse moved suggestively. Actually suggestively is the wrong word because as the clothing was so tight I could see everything. What I mean is that seeing her move back and forth like that from behind robbed my brain of any function, including intellectual conversation.
'Consider this doughnut. I want it. I want its fluffy goodness: the soft pillowy dough and the wet sweet innards. But I don't want

the extra pounds, both expense and weight. So what can I do, my desires are at war?'
'Just eat the doughnut?' I said.
'So the doughnut,' he continued unheeding. 'Is it through a lack of willpower that I give in, or lack of insight? For intellectualists such as Aquinas it is always a deficiency of understanding: we always do what we think is good. So to overcome temptation we have to get a better knowledge of what is good for us. For the voluntarists such as the Scotus the will is always free to choose between good and bad, we can do bad things for us even if we are fully aware of how bad they are for us.'
'Are you going to have it or not?'
'The mechanics of temptation probably lie somewhere between intellect and will: in the imagination where they are fused. In our thought lives. In our fantasies. As Thomas a Kempis put it: "at first it is a mere thought confronting the mind; then imagination paints it in stronger colours; only after that do we take pleasure in it, and the will makes a false move, and we give our assent."'
'The sauce is dripping on my hand.'
'Or,' he continued, 'perhaps the key thing is opportunity. If the temptation is put across your path you are powerless. But if you can avoid encountering the temptation in the first place then that is the best thing: if you eye leads you to sin, cut it out!'
'We could cut it in half if you want.'
'After all that, I don't think I really want the doughnut, you can have it.'
'Thanks, looks great.'
'I know what I want,' said Crichton, but he wasn't looking at the doughnut.
(Just in case you didn't get that subtle reference, let me be explicit: he was looking at Rice's arse. He couldn't take his eyes off her tight arse for the whole conversation. I think Crichton fancies Rice.)

6 - PUBIC MINISTRY BEGINS

Commentary

In this section Jesus begins his pubic ministry; calling disciples and setting forth his message of repentance and the Kingdom.

In my own way I like to think of my fellow departmental workers as my followers, for they are all considerably my juniors. Naturally there is some overlap in our work, but as the senior member of the group I have a certain *je ne sais croissant.* But indubiously I am the leader of the group, if not officially then by common custom. It is disturbing then when others do not respect my authority.

Take, for instance, the following occurrence. The time had come for submissions for the Stott-Scott Medallion. Now the Scott-Stott Medallion is the most prestigious award within the academic community based around the study of religion. Set up by the gay lovers (and banana magnates) Scott and Stott in 1909 it is given every five years and comes with a one million pound prize. Though of course it is the honour above all that counts: it is the one thing to show that you are really objectively better than others. Anyway, our departmental submission for the Scott-Stott award was due.

There is only one permitted submission for each institution and naturally I proposed that it would be my life's work on the Lost Gospel. My swan song of recognition. But no, Crichton put forward his project on Fragments of Faith, a piece of work whose ideas needless to say are all stolen from my own work. He is nothing but a second rate thief. That award belongs to me by right. But they all backed him.

Returning to the passage above, the key message Jesus has come to inseminate is that of repentance and the Kingdom of God, the sphere of influence of which he is the King. Repentance is

somewhat of an alien term for us post-hymenantic citizens, so for the general reader I will elaborate and illustrate. It was Martin Luther's rediscovery of this word which launched the culture shattering Reformation. Previously the word metanoia had been translated to mean to do penance (poenitentiam agite) which led to the system of sacramental sin management stemming from the Pope in which the sinner must do an act of penance to make up for their sin. Luther swept this all aside, insisting on repentance, the total turning of the heart in faith and trust to God; with the first of his 95 faeces reading:
When our Lord and Master Jesus Christ said '"Repent," he intended that the entire life of believers should be repentance.'

Repentance is the dramatic turning away from sin which is at the core of Christ's message. So similarly in our departmental situation repentance would mean Crichton retracting his submission to the Scott-Scott medal.

I will probably be able to use some photos I had previously bought to blackmail the Departmental Head at Cambridge to ensure that I can be entered through another institution. But I shouldn't have to.

7 - THE SERMON ON THE MOUNT

Commentary

Devins is the expert on the Sermon on the Mount in our group, though predictably his conclusions are obnoxiously wholesome. It is worth quoting him, I suppose, so you can taste his saccharine tang for yourselves:

> The beatitudes introduce the idea that the realm of Jesus' rule is based on a different set of values to the world. The world with Jesus as king is, from our point of view, upside down, a reversal. In the new administration we are given a new definition of success: not comfort nor wealth nor power nor pleasure nor security. It is those that the world considers failures who are nearer to God and his reign. Indeed it is even the case that those who in desperation reach for God, find him close to them: he is a God who acts to the glory of his grace, lifting up the lowly and casting down the mighty.

It has always been my hope that a more constructive approach to interpretation of the scriptures could be taken than this rather petrified, ossified archaeological digging of the text. For Devins it is all rather simple: God has spoken and shown what he is like, we must listen to the original communication asking the questions of the text what? how? and why? to recover the author's intent. But rather than this view of scripture as a window onto God, I have always seen scripture as something of a mirror. A human creation that can enrich our understanding of ourselves. (Mirrors are awfully useful, after all. Only the other day I found a speck of broccoli in my teeth from dinner a week back and was able to retrieve it.) Key to scripture as mirror is this: there is not any one meaning, just as what a mirror shows depends upon who is before it. So we can live with a multivalent text. So for instance in relation to the Sermon on the Mount:

Happy are the poor in spirit

Could mean that in general poor people are happier than rich people OR that in the future Jesus will turn things around so that poor people will be happy, even though they aren't at the moment OR that those who are humble in spirit are the ones who will come into Jesus' secret membership club of the kingdom and follow him OR that Jesus is bringing in a new set of values to contrast with the world OR the fact that it can be really satisfying to be miserable sometimes OR it's somehow great to be a limp-wristed, spineless shadow of a person OR several of these at the same time. The wonderful thing is that there is no right or wrong answers. No ultimate objective truth. No meaning except that which you can create from your own mind and fancy. What we get is simply our own thoughts and values reflected back at ourselves. Which, you must agree, is much better and more creative than those prissy Christians harping on about right and wrong and murder and so on. Just get over it.

8 - JESUS AND WOMEN

Translation

And Mary Magdalene came to him and wiped his feet with her hair. And Jesus said: Truely, truely I say to you: I appreciate the beauty of women. You cannot deny that when you see the body of an attractive woman, you feel the goodness of erotic desire.

Commentary

Von Wanque identifies these fragments as key in his magisterial work *Sex and the Saviour*, as showing us the more intimate side of Jesus of Nazareth. Sex is rehabilitated as always good, the last bastion of the transcendent we have left, a graced presence to experience (except rape and paedos obviously).

It is such a shame the world still in many ways treats sex as something dirty, to be performed behind closed doors. Take Devins for instance. He is single but believes from the Bible that he should stay celibate as he is unmarried. And he has a lovely cock (I saw when we were in neighbouring urinals), it is such a pity to see it go to waste. Similarly, it was a shame to see my entry banned for indecency from the competition of the Limerick Study Centre:

There was a young woman called Lydia,
Who had an unwanted sex phobia.
But then she was cured,
And went off abroad;
And ended up catching chlamydia.

I had hoped the world had moved beyond seeing sex as something puerile. I suggested as much to Rice, who I admit I have a soft spot for:
"In our age of equality and openness we should not feel ashamed of our sexuality but celebrate it," I said.
"What do you mean?" she asked.

"For instance, there is no reason why you should not show me your tits. Just lift up your top. Go on, show me your tits." Suffice to say, she didn't. But they are glorious and make me want to weep (her boobs). Again, why should we lock away beauty?

Naturally it is Augustine, that great doctor of desire, who has the most interesting things to say on this topic. For the urges within us can rarely be tangled apart. Who can say, for instance, whether desires for a tight-arsed colleague are, indeed, for total absorption into that blissful vessel, or whether they are yearnings for a deeper completion and ecstacy than can be provided in the flesh? Is sexuality subsumed in spirituality, or sublimated, or even is spirituality a repressed sexuality? Augustine himself always liked a nice pair (pear?), but was always troubled by the thought that we can be overcome by our darker desires and controlled by them. For him the answer came in a stronger desire, the desire for God. He has this comingling of sublime prayer and embarrassment about erections. It says a lot that he is the most influential theologian of the Western Church.

9 - JESUS PRAYS

Translation
Jesus leaves the crowds and heads off to pray.

Commentary
Prayer is, naturally - or unnaturally - one of those activities which we all catch ourselves engaging in from time to time, slipping into it without thinking. Such as picking your nose. And equally as distasteful (if you happen to taste the snot you will know what I mean).

It is characteristic for the uptight repressed Christian to press upon others the requirement to leave themselves behind: to concentrate the mind purely upon the wellbeing of others and the so called splendours of God, in the activity known as prayer. Fortunately humans are not capable of thinking of anything other than themselves for more than two and a half minutes in a row, so this attempt to rob us of our self-possession is limited in power.

Nevertheless, one must be wary of prayer. Consider for instance George Herbert who paints a pretty picture of this quieting of the web of thought so that something else can steal away the nous:

Prayer, the Churche's banquet, Angels' Age
God's breath in man returning to his birth,
The soul in paraphrase, heart in pilgrimage,
The Christian plunnet sounding heav'n and earth;

The poem goes on further but I can't bear to transcribe any more. Sickening.

Devins once told me that he prays for me. I can't imagine for what. I can think of nothing so monstrous as prayer.

It all reminds me of the occasion I attended an interfaith symposium on prayer. Although not what might be called a mainstream Christian, I was nevertheless invited as a senior scholar of religion. The topic had got onto prayer as a taste of heaven, and it was at this point that I made my contribution to the discussion:
'Aren't you Muslims meant to have seven virgins in heaven?'
'In the Arabic text-'
'Because the seven virgins, it is almost enough to make someone convert. You don't get anything that good with anything else. But I was wondering. I take it as read that they are virgins in the matter of vaginal penetration. But tell me this, because it's a dealbreaker, are they titwank virgins?'
'I'm sorry I don't understand what you're asking?'
'I am asking if they have made a sandwich, known a-'
'I think that it is metaphorical,' someone rudely interrupted.
'Because I would actually be open to more experienced women, so long as there were seven of them. For instance, in this city there was a woman whose hand was insured for ten million pounds because of what she could do with it. She could have you in paroxysms, a quiverring mass of nerves twanging. Of course she tried to claim the insurance money by severing the hand and got sepsis and died. Quite unfortunate.'

There was a silence. This often happens, I find, when groups become daunted by my intellect and incisive comments.

Of course even though Muslimhood has its advantages, in some ways I really am more of a Jew than anything else thanks to my accidental circumcision. It was the Jewish Heritage Museum as a teenager and there was this contraption with a hole, a sort of penile guillotine, and the opening - in a way - invited me to enter it, as I find penis shaped holes tend to do. One slip of the hand later and I became practically Jewish. I am veritably interfaith in many ways.

10 - PARABLES

Commentary

I too have done my duty as a good samaritan.

I was never certain whether Martin was his first name or his surname. He was originally from Newcastle, and perhaps that is all you need to know.

I met him in a layby off the A12 near Blythburgh. A yellow speed camera had been blown up into a blackened heap of twisted metal and there was a police car beside it which caught my attention. Martin had been stopped there by the police and was handcuffed. I decided to lend my assistance, rather than pass by one the other side like so many other hapless motorists.
'You are arrested for the destruction of speed cameras and for pig rape,' the officers said.
'It was consensual,' said Martin.
'Convenient that the camera is no longer around to verify that.'

'What's been going on?' I asked.
'There has been a tip-off,' said the officer. 'What we have done is finally catch the notorious speed camera assasin red-handed. Sixteen counts of arson over the last three years, speed cameras all over the Eastern Counties destroyed in a variety of ways, including one mobile unit. But he got cocky didn't he. Got sloppy. Lazy. Wanted to see the destruction with his own eyes. Abused a pig whilst he was waiting, he was that complacent. And we finally nabbed him.'
Overcome by compassion I decided to intervene to prevent the criminalisation of this poor man.
'I am sure there has been a misunderstanding,' I said, shaking the officer's hand and slipping him a crisp £50 note. Say what you like about the Suffolk Constabulary, they do the right thing when it counts. Martin got off with a warning and in thanks he took me to his place.

His dwelling is mostly a workshop where he devises his ingenious contraptions. He showed me around this mechanical wonderland. Martin is something of a guerilla justice warrior. Mainly concentrating upon the destruction of speed cameras across East Anglia he also has a sideline in porcine romancing, and is in much demand during insemination season.

The workshop was like a museum of exquisite destruction and I was given a tour. Here were the timed incendiary devices for the speed camera. There are the clockwork pigeons that allow him to spy out ahead. In the corner are the smoking plumes to provide any necessary distractions. On the worktop are the acid pellets which can dissolve a camera. And finally in the centre is his favourite contraption, the one he used to blow up the mobile speed monitoring unit. It is made of a large metal X which can clamp onto a moving car or van, and then a long wire which is attached to a super-strength battery: when the X is sprung or hurled and the switch is flipped a large current passes through which ignites the fuel in the petrol tank and creates a huge exploding fireball. Wonderful.

Martin invited me to join his campaign for the right to travel any speed he wishes without being caught. Although sympathetic, I am a man of thought not action. I said I would be thinking of him.

12 - THE CHURCH

Commentary

Attending church where necessary (funerals weddings university ceremonies) is always such an excruciating drag.

I find any excuse to take a breather from the ceremony. So normally whilst in a church I have to step outside at some point and have a fag. Now I am not usually that way inclined, but it is a welcome break from a church service. And I usually find that Church of England vicars have a couple of fags tucked away somewhere in the church. One time I even saw a fag through the vicarage window and I reached in and had it.

Anyway, leaning against the flinted buttresses, I was having this fag outside the church and who should come around the corner but the vicar, clutching a bottle of strong cider. He joined me against the wall. I imagine the Reader must have been giving the sermon on this occasion.

'Can't abide it,' he said. 'The parishioners are revolting. Bellends. Pricks. Dicks. Dongs. Cocks. Schlongs. Todgers. Phalluses. Penises. Wangs. Willies. Arses. Knobs. Tossers.'

'Any more?'

'Yes. Pusseys. Fannys. Mingers.'

'This is getting a little tedious now for-'

'Arseholes. Pissfaces. Fartfaces. Failfaces. Crapmunchers.'

'Let me stop you there,' I said. 'It's not particularly clever or funny to reel off a list of obscene language, you shit.'

'It is a little bit funny. But I suppose you're right,' the limp-wristed cleric continued. 'Still, they're the most terrible wankers.'

'I don't know, the most terrible wanker is called Crichton and he works at my college.' I use the word (wanker), advisedly, in an analogical manner. There is actually nothing wrong with autoeroticism.

'Surely it can't be all that bad,' I continued. 'Isn't the church meant to be...I don't know some mystical thing.'

'The church is made of people like Ms. Timms with halitosis, and Sam Evans who has been clinically depressed for thirty years and Mrs. Foggins who is a control freak. Actually there are a lot of control freaks.'

'But surely some of your theologians have sugar coated the concept of church into some grand thing.'

'Sure, take your pick: bride of Christ, body of Christ, spiritual temple, ship of faith and so on. What was it that CS Lewis said about the Church: 'spread out through all time and space and rooted in eternity, terrible as an army with banners.'

'Having a bride who is your own body sounds like autoeroticism to me.'

'Well the Reader will be drawing to a close now, I better be making my way back.'

As I finished off I realised that if Rice was the church and I was Jesus we would have some good autoeroticism together, if you know what I mean. (We would have sex.)

13 - OPPOSITION

Commentary

Jesus here enters his own personal Slough of Despond, reminiscent of Gethsemane. Bunyan, describing the Slough, talks of the fears and doubts and discouragements of that mirey valley. In his so-called mission of taking on the sin of the human race upon himself, it is not surprising therefore that Christ too had to trudge through its bog ridden slough that is the burden of sin.

Nobody enjoys Slough. Or wants to be there. Consider, for instance, the famous lines of Betjeman: 'Come friendly bombs and fall on Slough.' I went through on a train once. It was enough.

In contrast Betjeman was of course a great lover of East Anglia, our own garden of paradise. I concur with Betjeman on the glories of this corner of creation. So let us sing an ode to East Anglia; dawn mirrored in the waves; the shingle swept shores; ancient Kingdom of Canute, Roman capital and ruins and forts; Saxon churches burial mounds treasure; castles of war and a house in the clouds; pink washed walls and timber beams; meres bright and deep; sluggish rivers with mud stinking banks; fenland with rushes and warbling birds; orange cliffs pocked with nests; the A12 road a shining snake slithering through Eden; twisting lanes kissed with hawthorne honeysuckle trod by tractors; atom splitting domes and disused airfields; pine monocrops with UFO sightings; apples and crab and turkeys and pigs; container port and high street shops; sugar and hops and sun yellowed crops; visions of Mary and locked-in nuns; twilight bats on the backs; spiders and morning mists; the blast of the Siberian wind blowing unhindered across the wash and the wetlands and down cobbled streets of learning; the isle of eels floating on the fens; sunken cities with tide tolled bells; clay rolled fields, hill-less horizontals and flat expanse; the open sky;

the cold north sea. Did I mention tractors? Commuting on the A12 I regularly see and appreciate such beauty, travelling from Sutton to Dunwich. One sight that regularly mars my enjoyment is the view of Crichton's old Honda, as he travels on a similar route. I would rather not have to think of him. So I have developed a strict routine to avoid his presence, for I have precisely mapped his own journey over a few months:

8.08am - joins the A12 at Woodbridge
8.14am - crosses the Deben at Ufford on the A12
8.15am - passes Wickham Market turnoff
8.19am - Little Glemham
8.23am - Stratford St Andrew service station
8.26am - passes Friday Street turnoff
8.31am - takes the Dunwich Road at Saxmundham
8.45am - arrive in Dunwich
8.49am - arrive at Cromwell College and park
8.51am - wait for coffee outside our department
8.54am - enter the department
8.55am - crossword in common room with Rice
9.07am - starts work late. Wanker.

14 - THE END OF THE WORLD

Commentary

We tend to be interested in what happens to us after we die, choosing from the mezze menu of (1) biological dissolution (2) reincarnation (3) an afterlife, more or less pleasurable. The scriptures, including the Lost Gospel, are more interested in the Day of the Lord; with our individual destinies relegated into the shadowy background. The Day of the Lord is put simply the End of the World, the time set when God is to decisively intervene and all his promises will be cashed in. It is perhaps a sign for us to broaden our vision from the personal, even the cultural, to take into account the cosmological and ecological.

For the end of the world is nigh. We are told, reliably, that the reduction of biodiversity and use of resources by humanity means that a sixth great wave of extinction is underway. The irony is not that life will die out but that human existence will be made much more precarious. As Rupert Chytt writes, 'Biodiversity has halved in the last hundred years. Rather than correcting the decline we are speeding up. Impact of the Anthropocene on wild habitat means that in the next twenty years we are due to lose that same half again. Add on top of that the release of carbon into the atmosphere it is a wonder that we don't all blow our brains out in despair.' Of course Chytt famously went on to do just that.

Religious Conservatives may not worry about the exploitation and destruction of the world. After all they say it is to be replaced by a brand new one. Hand wringing conservations may wish for environmental protection but try to make others pay the necessary cost of economic stunting for this to happen. Jesus' view of the End is much more realistic.

Riven with inescapable selfishness, the only way for any sort of future is for God to intervene. He will have to renew and restore and revivify. It will not be another world created out of nothing but a renovated version of this world. For it is this world that is going to be renewed with its canyons and forests and sewers and beaches and gas-giants and toenails and waterfalls and skyscrapers and snails and symphonies and dodos (though probably not dildos). The plan is not so much a demolition as a refurbishment.

Such as when I attempted to put a replacement gasket onto my beat up old Land Rover. When things went wrong I did not seek to get an entirely new replacement car, such as one of those hybrids, but patched up the old. Renewal, recycling and sustainability in action.

Talking of cars, I think there might be something shady going on between Rice and Crichton. He has taken to giving her a lift into work most days.

15 - TRIUMPHAL ENTRY

We all awaited eagerly the Press Conference for the Stott-Stott Medallion, broadcast on the Academics Anonymous channel online. The entire Arts faculty of Cromwell College gathered, except Crichton who had phoned in with a stomach bug. Now the hour had come for my elevation. Now the hour of my glorification.

On the screen we saw the panel beginning their spiel. My bladder pressed against me urgently. Not long to wait now:
'We are proud to announce this year's Scott-Stott award,' the chair of the panel said. 'A breakthrough in early Christianities and the interaction between the pseudo and actual, making enormous contributions at Dunwich University, all of us have been thoroughly impressed by-'
Yes yes yes yes. It was true. It was me. Finally. I was weeping. I was laughing. I think I was having an orgasm. I won.
'And so we announce Richard Crichton as the winner.'

Emptiness. Complete emptiness as I watched that toad enter the camera frame. I watched mute as the medallion was placed around his neck. There was deafening cheering and whooping and applause from all around me as I stumbled to a chair. He gave his acceptance speech but I couldn't hear any of it. There was only this high pitched ringing noise in my ears and I felt so dizzy. I felt the hot flush which meant I had pissed myself. I put my head between my urine-soaked knees and tried to breathe.

Devins tried to take me aside for a little chat, but I was having none of it. I wasn't going to give him the satisfaction.

The next day Crichton drove into work in a brand new Honda.

16 - BETRAYAL

Following his reception of the Stott-Scott prize, Crichton threw a party in his elegant Edwardian townhouse, and everyone was invited. After typical drinks party nonsense a glass was tapped for a speech.

'It is under false pretexts that I have invited you to this celebration party for my academic achievements' said Crichton. 'Because this is not a work party but an engagement party." At this he drew Rice to himself, the fox, and they briefly kissed. There was a cheer and applause and Rice showed the rock on her finger to admirers.

So this was it then, an upcoming union.

What united my wife and I had been a mutual appreciation of her cunt. At the time we were both tweeded PhD students, and I must add she was rather under-confident, and both of us were dealing with paralysing doctorate frustration by wanking furiously in the stacks of the west wing of the library. One day we saw each other through the shelves in parallel aisles whilst twaddling ourselves and decided to half the effort involved. The shagging kept us together for many years but in the end she said that she outgrew me. It was probably the menopause.

What has the power to unite, and remain united? Theologians often speak of union with Christ in a similar vein to marriage; the Holy Spirit unites the soul to Christ so that everything that is his belongs to the believer, so that the believer shares all the benefits of being a son of the most high; just as an unequal marriage where all the riches and status of a prince is shared with a whoring pauper. Just as Crichton's wealth and success will become Rice's. Her body, her boobs, will become his. He will probably spray his spunk all over them (the boobs). Looking at

Crichton and Rice together I had to excuse myself and vomit a great quantity of canapes into a toilet bowl.

I could not tolerate this. I doused my head in cold water; I was feverish and shaking. My tight arsed hottie was to be lost to me forever, and worst of all to that complete cock Crichton who already stole my Scott-Stott award from me. I grit my teeth. No one could treat me this way without consequences. But what could I do? Suddenly I remembered Martin and his workshop.

Polishing the specks of vomit from my Badge of Honour, I travelled to the workshop under cover of night. There I laid hands upon the electric X and it's accoutrements, passing a fitful night, ready for decisive action in the morning.

17 - DEATH

Near Wickham Market there is a bridge over the A12, more of a deserted lane than a road, and it was here that I repaired early in the morning. Having picked up the electric X from Martin the previous night, I lay in wait.

The X itself, attached to the wire I held was ready to be disbursed. The X was attached via a long flexible wire to a high-intensity battery in the boot of my car. The wire, running through my belt, had a switch that I could press to turn on the current.

In the distance I could see Crichton's Honda approaching. I was certain that it was his. Now he would get all that was coming to him. The electric X would fall onto his car, ignite the fuel tank and BANG.

I timed it exactly right, just as I had planned. But I have never been the best thrower. When I was an undergraduate a long time ago I had been invited to a talk at the Christian Union by a fellow-student. The topic was the atonement. The speaker was outlining a version of Anselm from *Cur Deus Homo*. Namely, to preserve the beauty and order of the universe God will destroy sin and evil, and therefore demands a penalty for sin, satisfaction for the harm that has been done; but unwilling to see his creatures perish on account of their wayward hearts, another comes and makes satisfaction, bearing the penalty on their behalf, God incarnate, Jesus Christ; thus God's justice being satisfied and his love given on the cross, humans are made at one with God (at-one). All through this monologue, I became more and more angry at this abhorrent notion of blood-stained sacrifice being paraded in front of me, brutally clipping my bulletin-sheet into the most devastating paper aeroplane known to man. I resolved to throw it at the speaker at the crucial moment and ruin the talk. I was nineteen you must understand.

Reaching the climax of the talk, I flung the completed paper aeroplane as hard as I could. But as previously stated I am not very good at throwing, and the aeroplane did a loop-the-loop and poked me in the eye. A trip to A&E ensued.

But back to current events beside the dual-carriageway.

As I threw it, the X caught upon my Badge of Honour, and I fell over the bridge railing along with the X. I hung between bridge and A12, tangled up in wire from belt and badge and weighed down by the X dangling beneath. In danger of my life. I attempted to extricate myself from the snarled wire by wriggling and grasping. Unfortunately in the process the clothes on my bottom half must have been worked loose, for these spun through the air beneath me. But now I could climb back to safety on the bridge.

In all the tumult the equipment had been damaged, and as I laid a hand on the wire to raise myself up, a jolt ran through the wire. A large electric current passed through my body.

And I died.

18 - THE EMPTY TOMB

I died from electrocution, hanging mid-way between heaven and earth, half-naked, off a small intersection of the A12 dual-carriageway. It was not a metaphorical death. It was literal. Also I think I might have shat myself.

Now I am a ghost, or possibly a ghoul. I am not entirely cognisant of the difference between the two. My daily routine is little changed. I commute to work in the old Land Rover. I tap away on the computer, working on my research. I drink insipid tea from the machine in the staff room. I do my emails. I try to haunt Crichton, but he is merely convinced there is an unaccountable draught in his office. I try to play tricks on Devins but he seems to be surrounded by this blinding burning brightness and I can't get close. As for Rice, I can at least look down her top unhindered.

At the end of this Lost Gospel we are left with an empty tomb. After all the hope and work all that we are left with is emptiness. One can only imagine the soaring sense of victory that conventional Christians must have: Jesus is alive and risen from the dead, carrying life for the believer in his stead. What happiness, the defeat of the grave. But no, I cannot believe that the tomb was empty for a reason. All that remains is absence and loss. And emptiness in the tomb echoes the emptiness of my life.

Don't pretend you are any different from me, dearest slimeball, my reader, in all this. One sleepless night you died, and all that was left was the empty shell of life, an empty tomb. You walk and talk and check your social media feeds but inside is nothing, nothing at all. What remains for you is to stave off the darkness through endless distraction, a relentless Charybdis[1].

---

[1] Read Homer, you illiterate turd.

And that is the meaning, if anything, of this Lost Gospel. For it is not really the gospel which is lost, but us who have lost the religious transcendent, and we are haunted by the memory of our faded Christianity, the vanished tide.

SELECT BIBLIOGRAPHY

Crichton, David - *Fragments: fiction and faith in pseudo-gospels,* CUP 2016

Devins, Peter - *False Gospels*, Biblia Society Press, 2015

Lewis, C.S. - The Screwtape Letters

Lovecock, Ian - *Good Enough: Studies in self-validation.* PLATE 2017

Rice, Mary - *The lost voice of women,* Absentia Press 2010

Von Wanque, Heidrich - *Sex and the saviour: non-canonical perspectives*, Bristol Online Web Library 2008

INDEX

www.ingramcontent.com/pod-product-compliance
Ingram Content Group UK Ltd.
Pitfield, Milton Keynes, MK11 3LW, UK
UKHW020421250726
13967UKWH00007B/2752